Google+ Training

How To Utilise Google+ For Business to Generate Traffic, Leads & Clients

Sue Kennedy

First Printing, 2013

Printed in the United States of America

Income Disclaimer

This book contains business strategies, marketing methods and other business advice that, regardless of my own results and experience, may not produce the same results (or any results) for you. I make absolutely no guarantee, expressed or implied, that by following the advice below you will make any money or improve current profits, as there are several factors and variables that come into play regarding any given business.

Primarily, results will depend on the nature of the product or business model, the conditions of the marketplace, the experience of the individual, and situations and elements that are beyond your control.

As with any business endeavor, you assume all risk related to investment and money based on your own discretion and at your own potential expense.

Liability Disclaimer

By reading this book, you assume all risks associated with using the advice given herein, with a full understanding that you, solely, are responsible for anything that may occur as a result of putting this information into action in any way, and regardless of your interpretation of the advice.

You further agree that our company cannot be held responsible in any way for the success or failure of your business as a result of the information presented herein. It is your responsibility to conduct your own due diligence regarding the safe and successful operation of your business if you intend to apply any of our information in any way to your business operations.

Terms of Use

Google+ Training

How To Utilise Google+ For Business to Generate Traffic, Leads & Clients

Table of Contents

Introduction

"Everything should be made as simple as possible, but not simpler" ~ Albert Einstein

So what is Google+?

Google launched Google+ back in June 2011 and changed the social media landscape for the first time. Google+ was the new challenge for Facebook.

Right now Google+ is all the rage. This is why right now is the perfect time to get on the Google+ bandwagon. Just think about what might have happened to your business if you were in on the beginning of Facebook!

Nearly 50% of companies actually rate Google+ as an important tool for their business. In 2012, 15% of marketers got a customer from using Google, so it is no wonder that Google+ has attracted 500 million registered users that has now grown into the second largest social network as of January 2013.

Google chose the name Google+ as they want this product to become known as an extension of Google itself.

Google+ is basically a mixture of different social products and features.

- ~ **Stream - a newsfeed**
- ~ **Sparks - A recommendation engine**
- ~ **Hangouts – video chat feature**
- ~ **Circles – a way of managing your connections**
- ~ **Photos**

Google+ is an amazing opportunity for individuals and businesses in the next year. Start using this awesome tool and be lightyears ahead of your competition!

Google+ will be a vital "One Stop Shop" for your business marketing needs.

If you are like many others and believe that no one is using Google+, then please let me share some statistics with you:

- Google+ has grown to 400 million users in just over 12 months

- 100 million people are active each month on Google+
- 150 million people are active across all of Google each month
- 50% of these people sign in each day and spend up to 12 minutes per day just on their Google+ stream (this figure is up by 3 minutes from August 2012)
- Google+ is backed by one of the largest and most successful companies in the world
- The development and growth of Google+ is a priority for Google in the future
- Google+ is known as not just another social network, but a recommendations engine. The most important thing to remember here is that this recommendations engine is being integrated in the search results of Google. Imagine what this means for your business in the next six to twelve months!

The future of Google+ is very exciting for businesses.

AUTHORSHIP

"Words are a form of action, capable of influencing change"
~ Ingrid Bengis

An important point to remember is that if your business relies on Google as your major source of online traffic and revenue, then you need to develop your Google+ strategy as soon as possible.

One of these reasons is "Authorship". What is authorship you ask? It is basically the process in which you tell Google which content you have written yourself either on your website or on the web. Please see an example below of how the Authorship looks like:

As you can see in this image, it shows some interesting information that adds to your search results:

- It has an image of the author

- It has a "byline" that links to the author's Google+ profile, and
- It shows the author's credibility by listing how many people that author has in their Google+ circles

Having authorship linked will not have an enormous effect on your search rankings at the moment, but it will definitely help with your click through rates in the natural search results.

The following link shows you how to set up your authorship:

https://plus.google.com/authorship?partnerid=gplp0

AUTHOR RANK

What is Author Rank? This is actually really exciting and will be bigger than Panda and Penguin combined! Back in August 2005, a patent was filed that was called "Agent Rank". What this meant was that the patent would 'rank agents' dependent on the content they created.

Currently, authorship is the only rich snippet that appears in the search results, however, the term 'Author Rank' has been chosen over 'Agent Rank', which we should see as the next algorithm update from Google.

Is this a good thing? Of course it is, this means that we will get good quality content all the time and this will weed out the spammers – that has to be a good thing, wouldn't you agree?

Google knows that people want to read content that is written by credible and intelligent people therefore, using Author Rank will play a major part in their search alogoritms.

So how will Google factor the signals for Author Rank?

Apparently Google considers over 200 ranking factors when they determine where sites would rank in organic search, so it's likely that they will have plenty of signals when they calculate Author Rank. Following is a list of some of the factors Google will likely consider in their calculations:

- The average +1's and Google+ shares the author receives
- Reciprocal connections to high Author rank authors
- The average Page Rank of the author's content
- The level of engagement of the author's content of posts to Google+
- YouTube engagement/subscribers on authored videos
- The number of Google+ circles the author is in

- The number of authority sites an author has published content to
- Outside authority indication, eg a Wikipedia page
- The level of engagement of the author's content, relating to comments and responses from the author
- Published work on either Google Books or Google Scholar
- The number of important/authority metics on social networks that Google trust like Twitter, Linkedin, Slideshare etc.

To get underway, firstly set up your Google authorship, this will allow Google to assign you an initial Author Rank.

Start to write good high quality content and keep building on this each day.

Following are some great strategies to help you achieve the building of your Author Rank:

- Use Google+ consistently, because one of the ranking factors is your "in circles"
- Make sure you post updates a few times per day
- Make sure you check your feed and the global feed and be sure to +1 and comment on interesting stories. This not only makes the people that wrote the content happy, it

also adds to the conversation and can only be a benefit to you and your author rank

- Make sure you complete your "about" section and title properly. People will use this to determine if they should add you to their circles
- Find high-ranking authors and befriend them. Find them on Google+ and slowly and naturally build a relationship
- Promote your Google+ profile. It is the hub of your authorship. If your Google+ profile gets a high page rank (yes, it does have it's own page rank!) then when Author Rank launches you can be sure that your rank will be great
- Make sure that you don't just publish your content on your blog or website; get your content out to other places, for example, you could be a guest blogger, be sure to remember to select high quality sites when you are doing this

Of course you cannot build Author Rank overnight, nor should you, it should be a natural and gradual process. The following is a system that can help you build this ranking over time.

Here is your daily checklist to help improve your Author Rank:

- Check your Google+ feed at least five times and don't forget to interact

- Make sure you work on your weekly blog post each day
- Find high quality blogs that you would like to be a guest blogger and leave quality comments, this will start to build your relationship and visibility with the author of the blog
- Find two to three people on Google+ that you find interesting and circle them, and importantly, interact with their stories

Action Steps

1. Sign up for your Authorship
2. Sign into your Google+ account each day and interact
3. Write some content for your weekly blog
4. Find quality blogs to comment on
5. Find people of interest on Google+, circle them and interact with them

Getting Started with Google+

"Readers are plentiful, thinkers are rare"
~ Harriet Martineau

Firstly "TAKE AIM" - Before you set up your Profile, you really MUST define WHO your target market is.

Who is your target audience?

Who is your target client/customer?

Narrow down your market and find a niche, a niche you can create a specific marketing messages for.

This way you can build a great base of clients/customers through Google+ and expand from there.

To help you narrow down your target market, here are some questions you can ask yourself:

1. Who needs your product or service most? Why do they need it?

2. What kinds of people do you resonate with the best? What type of person would you like to attract to your business?

3. What is that person's typical age?

4. Where does that person generally live in relation to you? What areas can you serve? Which areas do you want to serve?

5. What is the typical gender of your target audience?

6. What is the typical income of your target audience?

7. What is your target audience's marital or family status?

8. What is the education level of your target audience?

9. What is your target audience's typical occupation(s)?

To access Google+ you need to have a Google Account.

- https://www.google.com/accounts/

Following is the screen where you need to sign up or sign in if you already have a Google account:

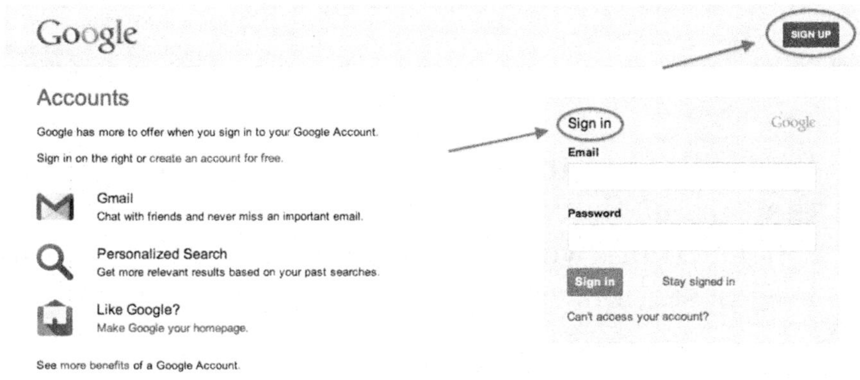

Your next step is to create your Google+ Profile.

Your profile page has five tabs:

~ *Posts*
~ *About*
~ *Photos*
~ *Videos*
~ *+ 1's*

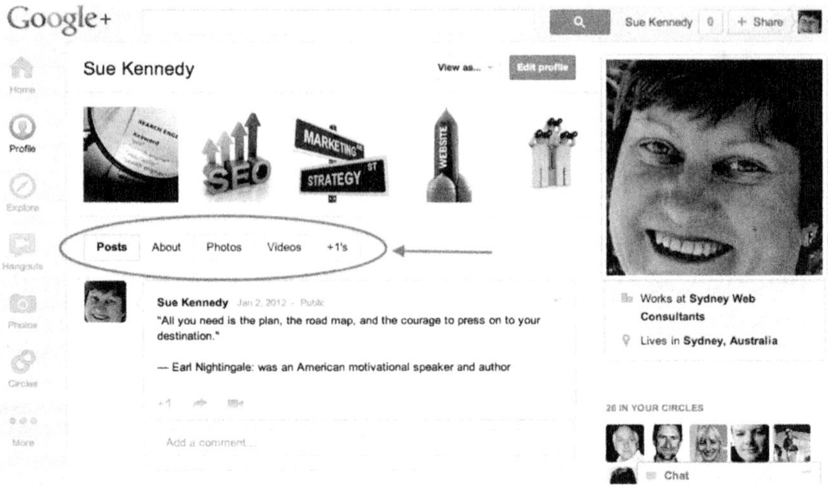

You will want to go into edit profile and fill out the various fields. This is located under the About tab. Currently you can add information in the following sections:

- ~ *Tagline*
- ~ *Introduction*
- ~ *Bragging Rights*
- ~ *Occupation*
- ~ *Employment*

The "Introduction" on your About page is the most important part of this page

We recommend you write 3 short paragraphs in this section. The first needs to be exciting enough for people to want to know you, next a little bit about what you do and finally a call to action

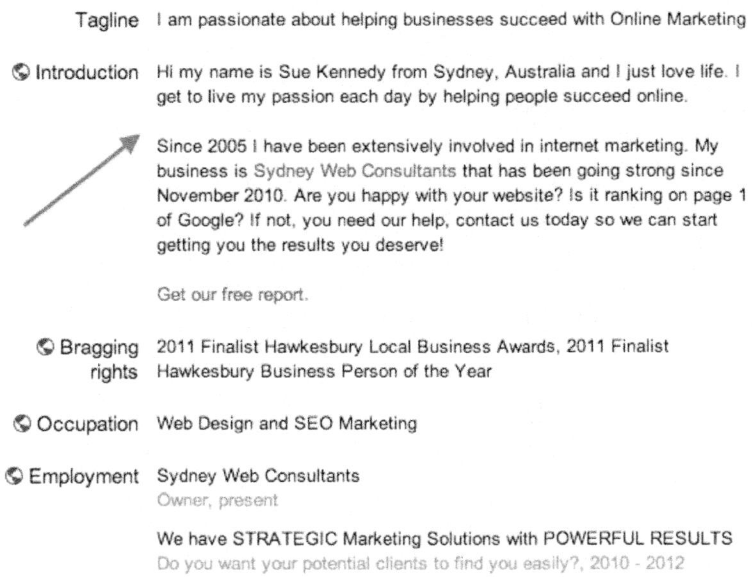

TIP: Make sure you rock the pop up box. When someone hoovers over your profile image in Google+ a little popup box displays. What if you could put your marketing message in here? Well guess what, you can. Go to your "About" page and click on "Edit Profile", scroll down to "Employment" and edit.

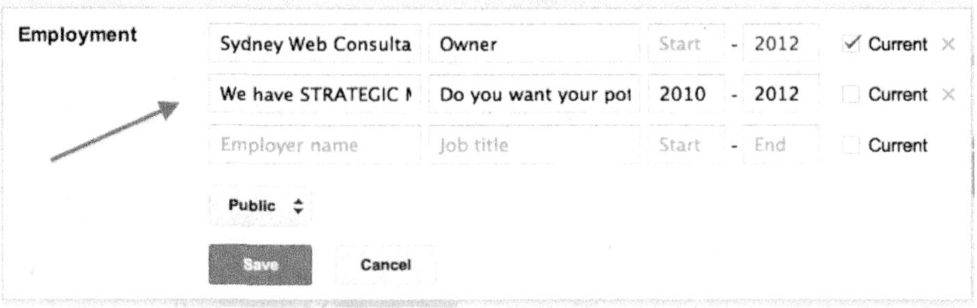

- ~ *Education*
- ~ *Places Lived*
- ~ *Home*
- ~ *Work*
- ~ *Relationship*
- ~ *Looking for*

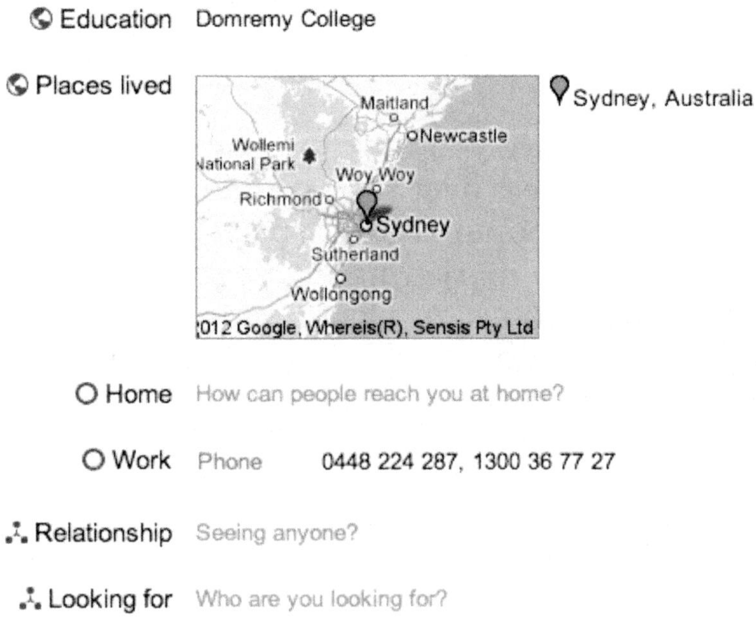

~ Gender
~ *Other names*
~ *Other Profiles*
~ *Contributor to*
~ *Links*

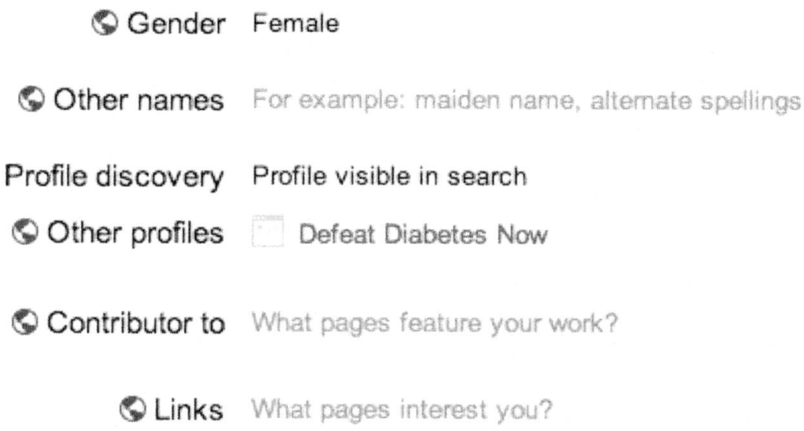

The Other Profiles and Link fields are important as it allows you to link to other profiles on the web. Plus you have the ability to add a custom link. So if you have a personal blog or website you can link directly to it.

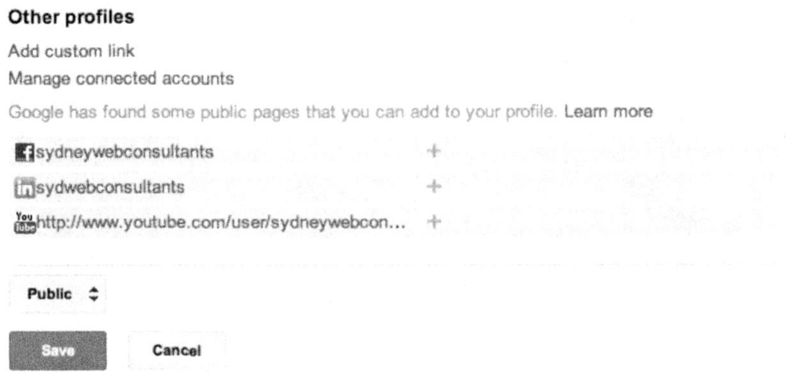

To enter custom links perform the following steps:

1. Sign in to your Google+ Profile
2. Click Edit Profile
3. Click on the About Tab
4. Click the Links section on the right hand side
5. To add a link that Google suggests simply click ADD to add a custom link
6. Click on ADD Custom Link
7. Enter the name and URL

8. Check the box that says 'this page is specifcally about me' if applicable

9. Click Save

10. You can change order of your links by dragging the link and re-organising your list

Action Steps

1. What are 4-5 keywords you think your business is about or what are people typing in when trying to find you?

____

____

____

____

____

2. What niche are you in?

____

3. What are the top 3 products or services you want people to know about?

____

____

____

4. What are 2-3 things you do better than your competitors?

5. What are your top 2-3 problems your customer has and how are you solving that?

6. Who needs your product or service most? Why do they need it?

7. What kinds of people do you resonate with the best? What type of person would you like to attract to your business?

8. What is that person's typical age?

9. Where does that person generally live in relation to you? What areas can you serve? Which areas do you want to serve?

10. What is the typical gender of your target audience?

11. What is the typical income of your target audience?

12. What is your target audience's marital or family status?

13. What is the education level of your target audience?

____

14. What is your target audience's typical occupation(s)?

____

____

15. Wite out your "Introduction". Remember it is 3 paragraphs long. The first paragraph needs to show your passion, the second paragraph describes what you do and the benefits you offer, and lastly, this paragraph is your call to action.

Google+ Privacy

"A business has to be involving, it has to be fun, and it has to exercise your creative instincts"
~ Richard Branson

To navigate to your privacy settings click on the gear icon in the upper right hand corner. Then go to Google+ Settings.

From here you can change all of your privacy settings by clicking on different links.

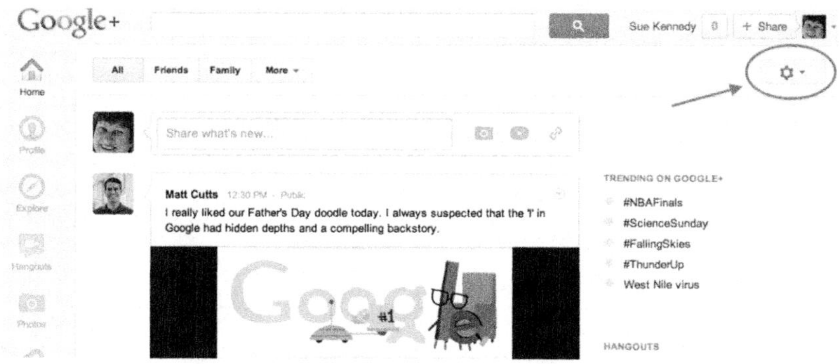

- Account
- Security

- Profile and Privacy
- Google+
- Products
- Language
- Data Liberation

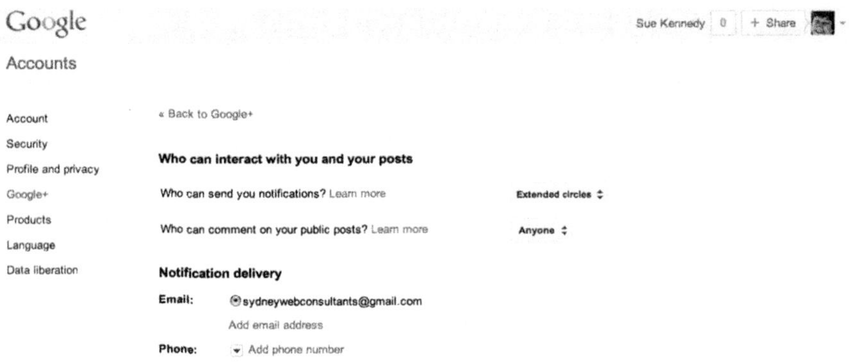

The Data Liberation tab allows you to download your data from specific services such as downloading your circles and contact information.

The Google+ Settings page allows you to add your email address and your mobile number. You can then select how and when you want to be notified when someone in your circles adds content.

Google has taken great steps to ensure that people can delete their accounts when they wish. They can simply download their information via the Data Liberation feature and delete their account.

ACTION STEPS

1. Go to your settings and make sure all your privacy settings are setup correctly

Google+ Circles

"Belief in oneself is one of the most important bricks in building any successful venture"
~ Lydia M. Child

This is the area that you really want to pay attention to and master. The best thing about Google+ is that you are given much more control over who can see your content.

Circles gives you the ability to send customised messages to a specified group of people.

By clicking on the Circle icon a new page is displayed with some existing circles. These include:

~ *Friends*
~ *Family*
~ *Acquaintances*
~ *Following*

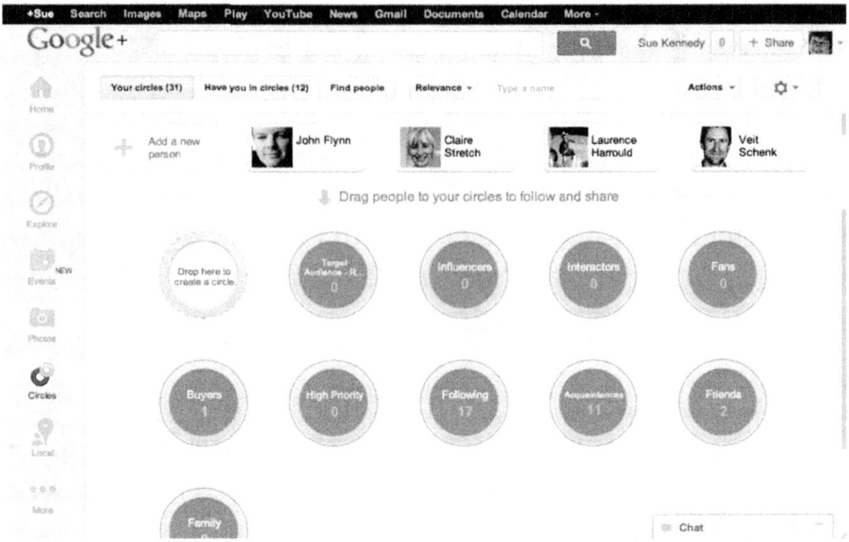

Plus you have the option of creating new circles.

To add someone into your circle you can simply drag and drop them into the appropriate circle. Google will suggest friends by using your Google contacts. You can also import your Facebook and Linkedin Connections, which will be shown shortly.

By clicking on the circle itself you can rename and organise your circle. You can add a description and even delete a circle if you wish.

The reason why Circles are so important are that they allow you to share different information with certain people. You can choose who sees what!

In order to be successful with Circles, you must have a strategy of setting up your fundamental Circles for your business. What we recommend for all types of businesses is to setup the following fundamental Six Circles: Influencers, Buyers, Raving Fans, Interactive, High Priority and Target Audience

Influencers Circle - These are iconic figures in your specific industry where you want to target clients from, these influential people have specific followers already and they could be interested in your products or services.

Interactors Circle - These are people interacting with you online. They are commenting, sharing, +1'ing your posts. It's very important to know who your online cheerleaders are.

Fans Circle - These are a higher level of interactors. These people are talking about you and your business. These people are always commenting about your posts. These people are actively following you and praising you on your work and efforts. These people are the BIG scratchers of your back! Look after them!

Buyers Circle - These are current or past clients/customers that have bought from you. Make sure you keep track of these people on Google+ as you want to make sure you interact with them. You need to stay front of mind to these people so next time you have a product or service offering they will be more than willing to purchase.

High Priority Circle - These are specific people that you would only keep in this circle for 4 to 6 weeks. These are potential influential people that you want to gain a relationship with, people that can benefit you and your business. Work really hard for these weeks and build a relationship with them. But it is advisable to only have 3 to 5 people in a given month.

Target Audience - Real Estate Agents Circle - This circle will change as you choose to target different audiences.

TIP: Make sure you put your circles in priority so when you post something, you can easily select from the dropdown box without having to scroll right to the bottom of the list.

Other Circles of interest that you can create is your own circle as you being the only member.

A draft Circle is another one that would be perfect if you are in the habit of writing long posts. Simply file them here until you are ready to post.

Another Circle that you could create is a Local circle and this could include any local business that you use. Or place people here who live in your neighbourhood, friends of your children, school info and more.

ACTION STEPS

1. Create all the circles mentioned in this chapter that relate to your business

Google+ Stream

"Success in business requires training and discipline and hard work. But if you're not frightened by these things, the opportunities are just as great today as they ever were"
~ David Rockefeller

The Stream feature is basically a newsfeed of the content shared by members of your circle.

The posts or photos with the most comments will normally stay at the top of the Stream. If you enjoy the post then you are encouraged to hit the +1 button.

At the top of each post there is a small arrow and by clicking this arrow you are shown some options. You can link to the post, mute the post, report abuse or block the person.

To update your status you simply type in a comment and then hit the share button. You then have the option of choosing who to share it with.

Once you have shared a post, a pop up appears with tips about your post. These will tell you things like how you can fix a typo in your post by clicking on the drop down arrow of each post.

You can choose to share text, a photo, links or a video. Google will automatically detect the link and allow you to choose a thumbnail for your post.

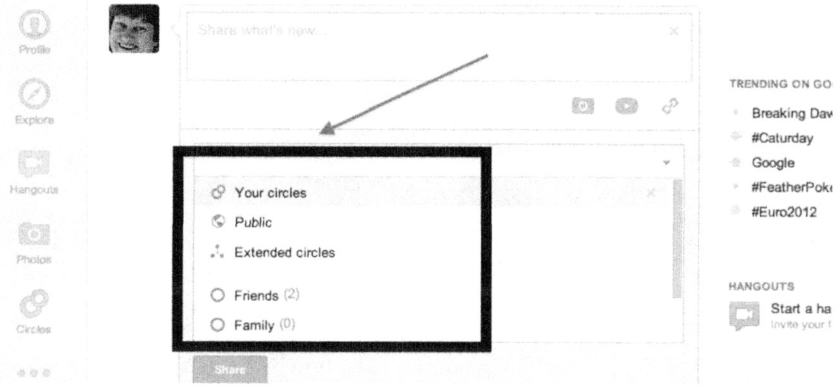

Your Stream page will also show suggestions of who you may want to include in your circles.

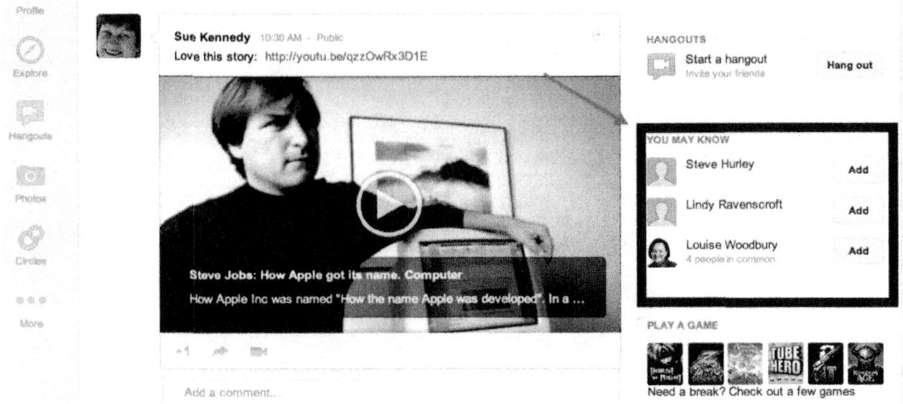

ACTION STEPS

1. Check your newsfeed and interact with your circles on a regular basis

Google + Sparks

"Long–range planning works best in the short term" ~ Doug Evelyn

Google Sparks is basically a content recommendation search engine. Sparks are your "areas of interest" in Google+.

Once you find something you like then you click the add button and this link is pinned underneath your Saved Searches link for easy navigation. You can also share this content with your Circles.

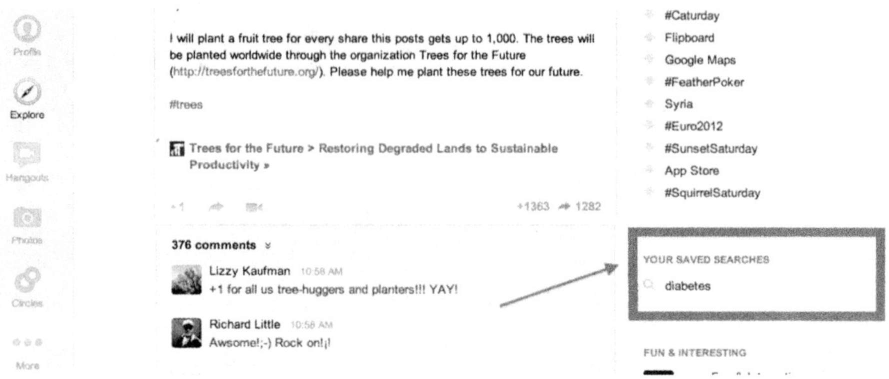

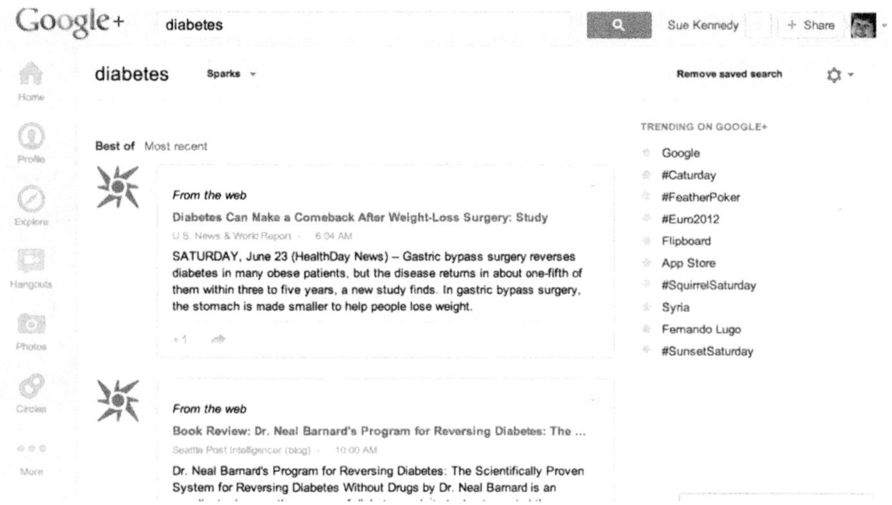

ACTION STEPS

1. Find some topics of interests and add them to your saved searches

Google+ Hangouts

"Good business leaders create a vision, articulate the vision, passionately own the vision, and relentlessly drive it to completion"
~ Jack Welch

The Hangout feature is on the right side navigation on your Stream page. Google Hangouts is a group video chat feature and you simply click on Hangouts to get started.

You can invite up to ten people to join in your Hangout and you can chat via microphone.

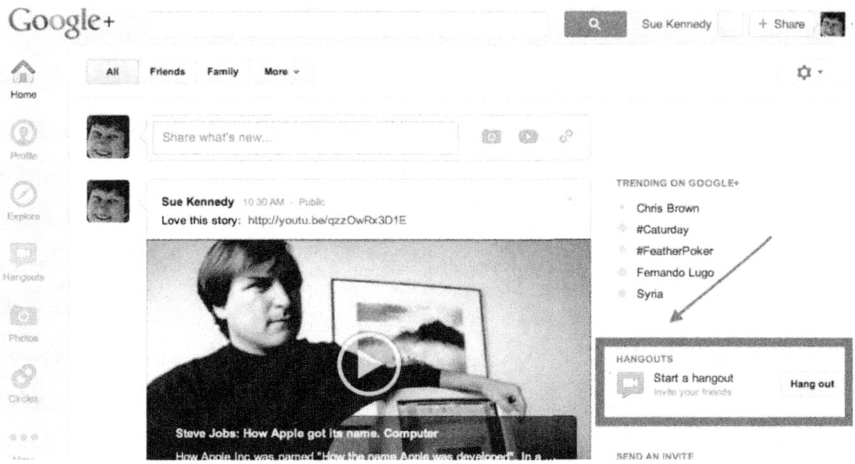

While engaged in a Hangout session the video automatically goes to the person who is talking.

There is also a group chat feature that can be enabled. One great feature is the ability to allow everyone in the Hangout to watch a YouTube video.

There are setting options, which allow you to adjust your mic, video, camera and additional features.

ACTION STEPS

1. Organise a hangout session with your friends or collegues

Google+ Photos

"Believe in yourself and you will be un-stoppable"
~ Emily Guay

Clicking on the Photo tab will show you pictures that people in your circles have uploaded. You can organise your photos to be viewed in different categories:

- ~ *Photos from your Circles*
- ~ *Photos from your Phone*
- ~ *Photos of You*
- ~ *Your Albums*

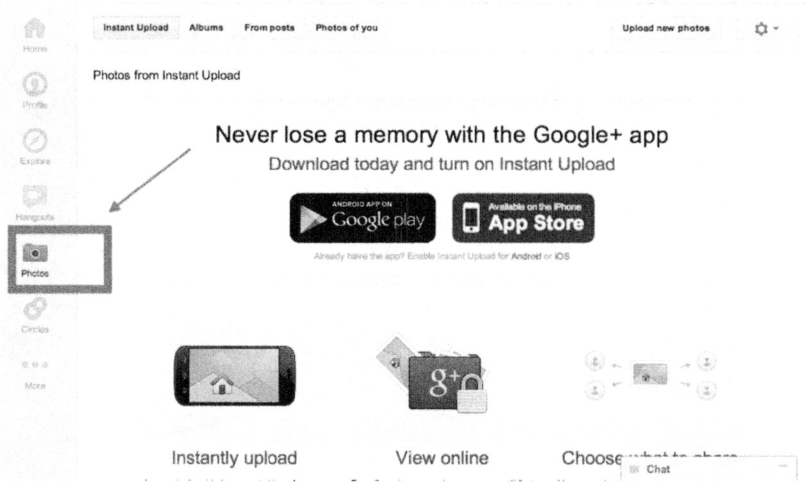

If you click on a photo it will bring up a slideshow feature, which will show any recent comments made on the photo. While in the slideshow view you can add tags and see features such as when the photo was taken and by what type of camera.

Once you are notified that you have been tagged you either accept or reject the tag.

The “Your Albums” section allows you to upload and create your own photo albums.

After you have uploaded your photos Google gives you the ability to edit them.

ACTION STEPS

1. Organise photos from your circles
2. Upload some of your photos and share the

Google+ Chrome Extensions

"The competitor to be feared is one who never bothers about you at all, but goes on making his own business better all the time"
~ Henry Ford

For anyone who uses Google Chrome there are some extensions which you can use to make using Google+ easier.

Beautify G+ is an extension that allows you to fix the left and right hand menus in place. This makes scrolling through your stream more manageable.

GPlus + Search adds an icon to the Chrome toolbar that allows you to search for Google+ content.

Usability Boost for Google+ changes the background of the posts to make them easier to read. This is great if you find reading your Stream hard on your eyes.

+Photo Zoom allows your photos to enlarge while hovering over the image for a certain length of time. This extension comes with settings so you can adjust the time length.

Replies and More for Google+ this adds a Reply to Author function to your posts. This extension automatically adds +name to your post or your comments. It also features a drop down box, which allows you to share to your linked accounts.

G+ Count in Title adds a counter to your Google+ page tab so you can see how many posts you have to view.

G+ Extended allows you to add shortcuts such as pressing 'e' to expand all the comments or 's' to share the comments.

Helper for Google+ allows you to receive desktop notifications and share your posts via Twitter. It has an audio alert button and a translate option.

+Comment Toggle allows you to hide or show comments depending upon how busy your Stream is.

Extended Share for Google+ allows you to quickly share with other sites such as LinkedIn, Facebook and Twitter.

ACTION STEPS

1. Try out the chrome extensions to see which ones work the best for you

Google+ Tips

"The important thing is not being afraid to take a chance. Remember, the greatest failure is to not try. Once you find something you love to do, be the best at doing it" ~ Debbi Fields

Here are some tips and tricks that we have found to make your Google+ experience more exciting and easier!

The following are font effects that you can use:

italic text = *italic text*

bold text = **bold text**

-strikethrough text- = ~~strikethrough text~~

*italic bold text* = ***italic bold text***

If you would like to tag a friend in one of your Google+ posts then all you have to do is simply type the @ or + and then start typing their name.

If you wish to scroll forwards in Google+ use the 'J' key and the 'K' key will allow you to scroll backwards.

- Every post should have a bolded title

- Always have short paragraphs

Make sure you "Bold" emotional words and words you want to stand out.

ACTION STEPS

1. Have a play with these tips and see how well they work for your business

Google+ Cheat Sheet

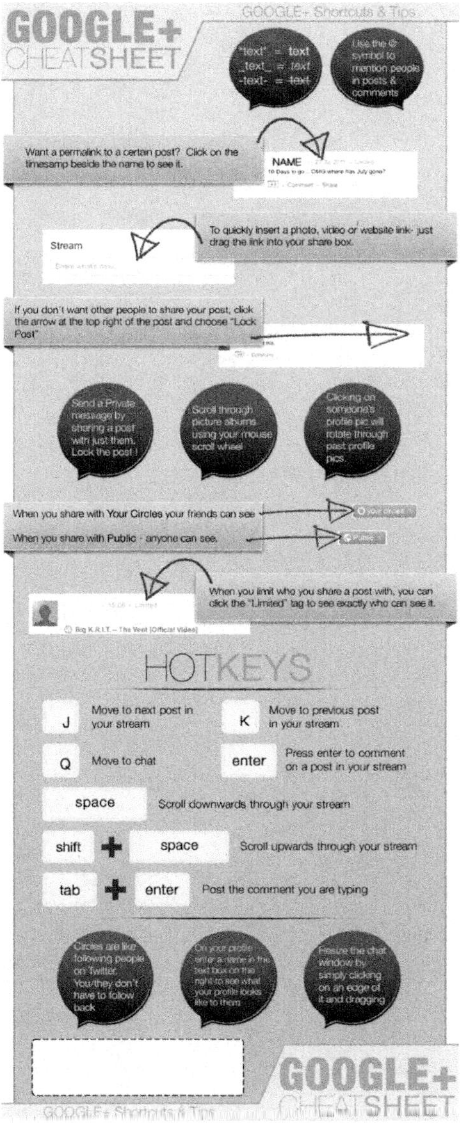

Transferring your Facebook Contacts

"Those who say it can not be done, should not interrupt those doing it"
~ Chinese Proverb

1. Download "Email Hunter", this is an extension for Chrome

2. Login to your Yahoo Account

3. Go to your "Mail" and click on "Contacts"

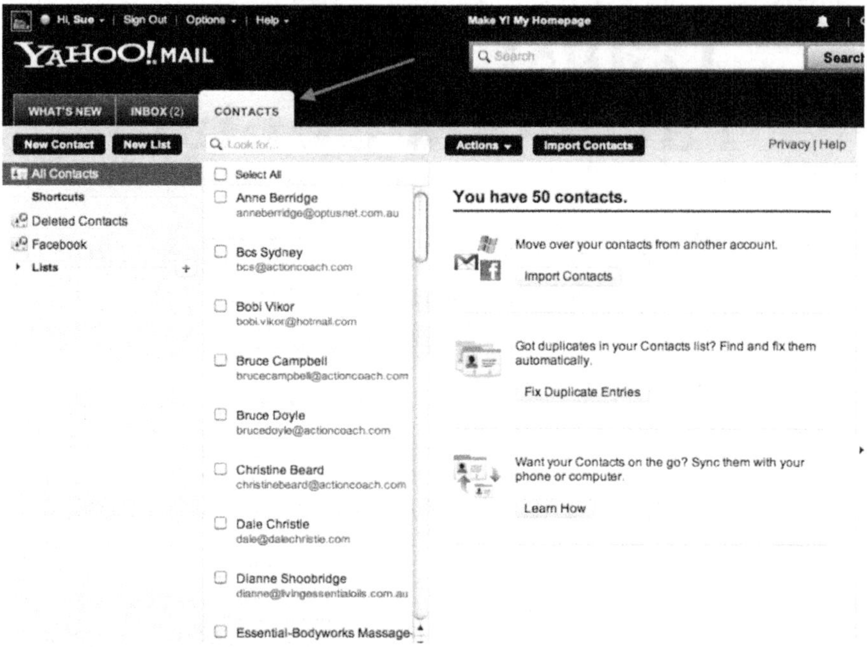
Hi, Sue
Sign Out
Options
Help
Make Y! My Homepage
YAHOO! MAIL
Search
WHAT'S NEW
INBOX (2)
CONTACTS
New Contact
New List
Look for...
Actions
Import Contacts
Privacy | Help
All Contacts
Shortcuts
Deleted Contacts
Facebook
Lists
Select All
Anne Berridge
anneberridge@optusnet.com.au
Bcs Sydney
bcs@actioncoach.com
Bobi Vikor
bobi.vikor@hotmail.com
Bruce Campbell
brucecampbell@actioncoach.com
Bruce Doyle
brucedoyle@actioncoach.com
Christine Beard
christinebeard@actioncoach.com
Dale Christie
dale@dalechristie.com
Dianne Shoobridge
dianne@livingessentialoils.com.au
Essential-Bodyworks Massage
You have 50 contacts.
Move over your contacts from another account.
Import Contacts
Got duplicates in your Contacts list? Find and fix them automatically.
Fix Duplicate Entries
Want your Contacts on the go? Sync them with your phone or computer.
Learn How

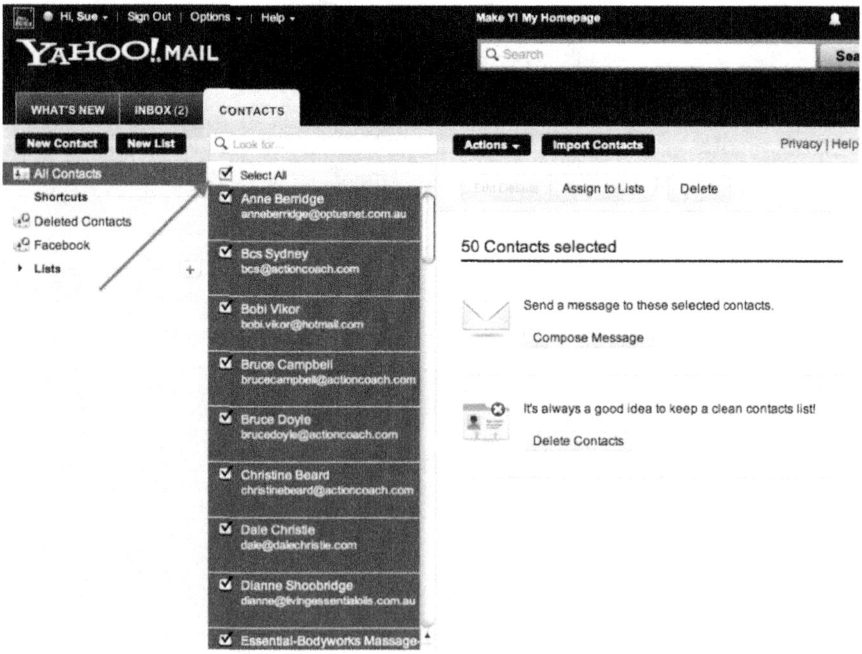
Hi, Sue
Sign Out
Options
Help
Make Y! My Homepage
YAHOO! MAIL
Search
WHAT'S NEW
INBOX (2)
CONTACTS
New Contact
New List
Look for...
Actions
Import Contacts
Privacy | Help
All Contacts
Shortcuts
Deleted Contacts
Facebook
Lists
Select All
Assign to Lists
Delete
Anne Berridge
anneberridge@optusnet.com.au
Bcs Sydney
bcs@actioncoach.com
Bobi Vikor
bobi.vikor@hotmail.com
Bruce Campbell
brucecampbell@actioncoach.com
Bruce Doyle
brucedoyle@actioncoach.com
Christine Beard
christinebeard@actioncoach.com
Dale Christie
dale@dalechristie.com
Dianne Shoobridge
dianne@livingessentialoils.com.au
Essential-Bodyworks Massage
50 Contacts selected
Send a message to these selected contacts.
Compose Message
It's always a good idea to keep a clean contacts list!
Delete Contacts

4. Select “All”

5. Select “Compose Email”

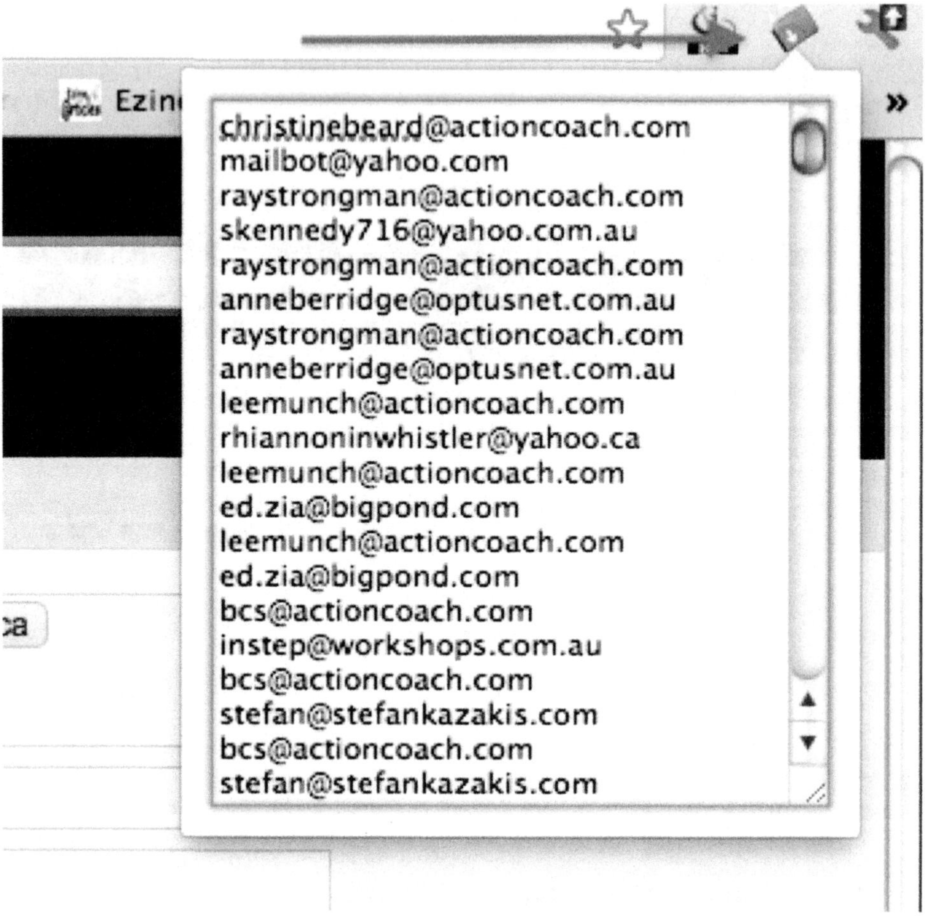

6. Click on “Email Hunter” in your toolbar

7. Copy addresses from the dropdown box

8. Go back to Google+

9. Go to your Gmail

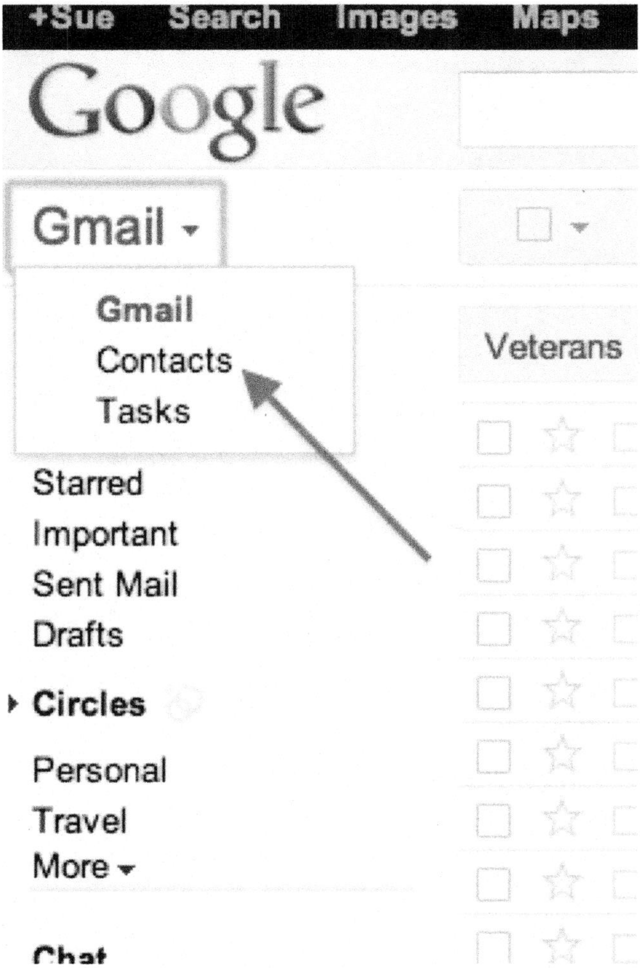

11. Copy the list of emails from "Email Hunter" into this box

12. Click on "Add"

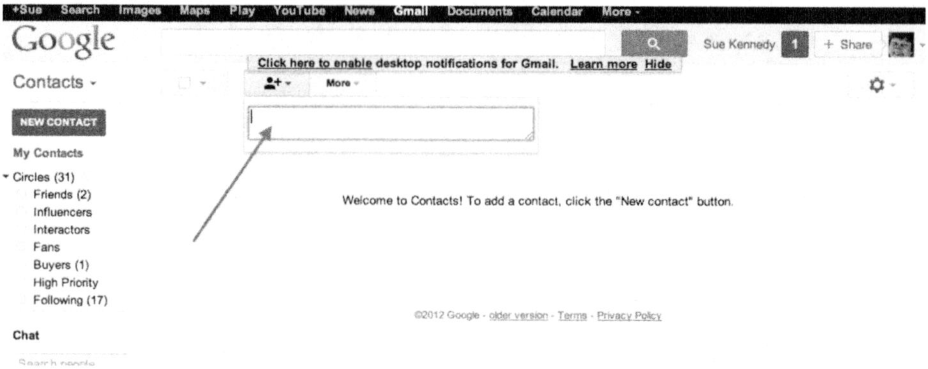

13. Go back to your Circles

14. Create a new circle called “Facebook Contacts”

15. Click on “All Suggestions”

16. Click on “Gmail”

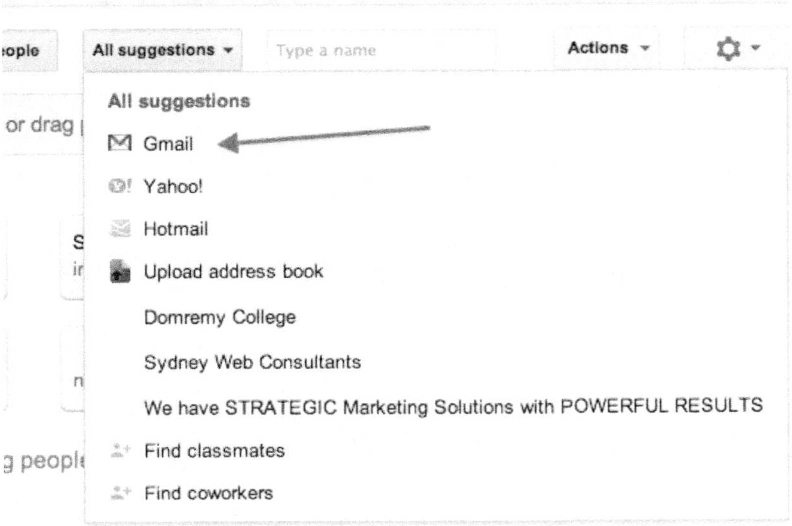

17. Select "All" your Facebook contacts

18. Drag them into your new Circle called "Facebook Contacts"

And from there if you would like to move them into other circles, please do so.

ACTION STEPS

1. Go through this chapter and transfer all your Facebook contacts

Transferring your LinkedIn contacts

"In the business world, everyone is paid in two coins: cash and experience. Take the experience first; the cash will come later" ~ Harold Geneen

1. Sign in to your LinkedIn Profile

2. Select "Contacts"

3. Select "All"

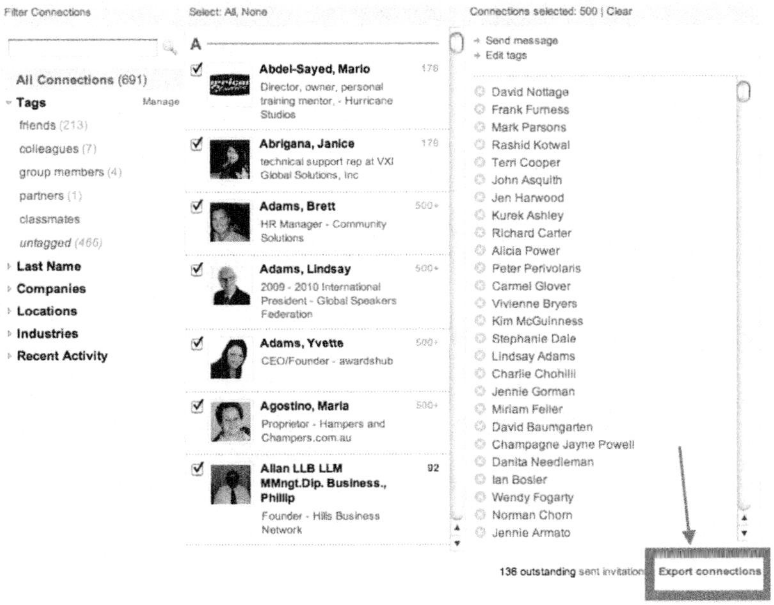

4. Export Contacts

5. Select where you want to export to

6. Enter in Captcha code

7. Go back to Google+ Circles

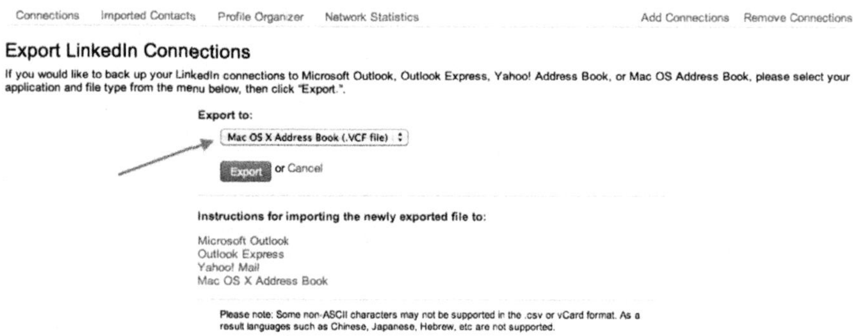

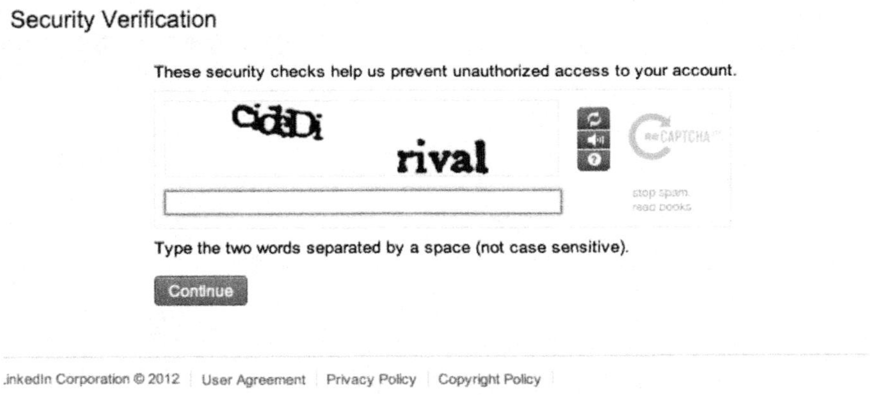

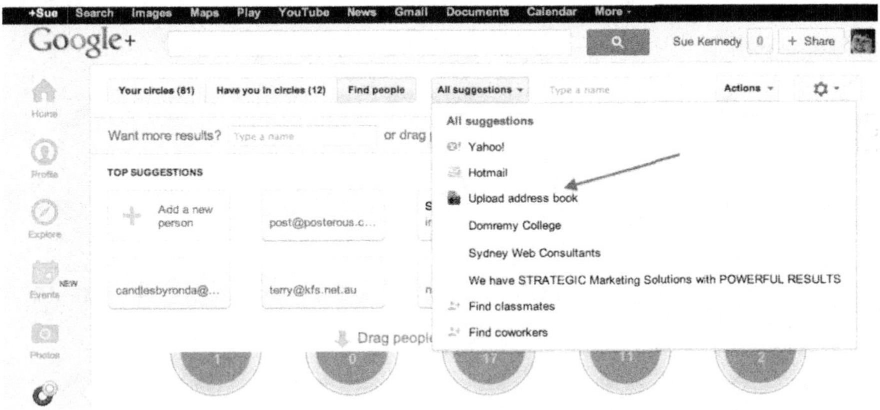

8. Upload to your Address Book

9. Go to Downloads

10. Select the LinkedIn file

11. Upload

12. Create a circle and copy your connections

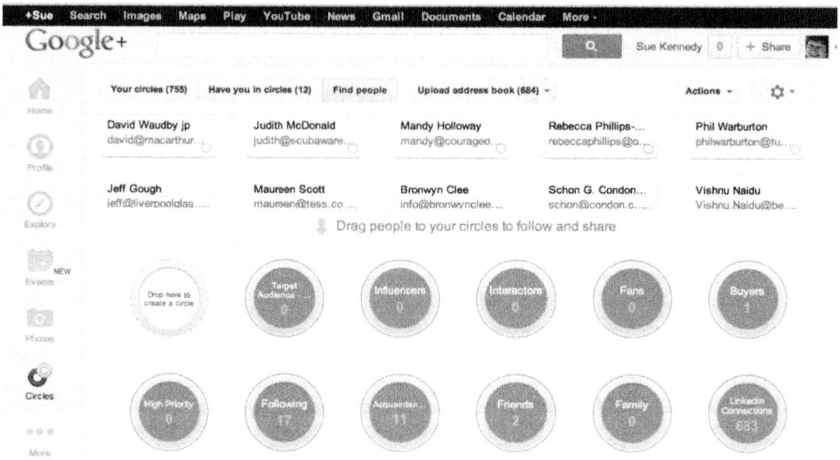

ACTION STEPS

1. Go through this chapter and transfer all your linkedIn connections

Content for your Posts

"Whatever the mind of man can conceive and believe, it can achieve. Thoughts are things! And powerful things at that, when mixed with definiteness of purpose, and burning desire, can be translated into riches" --~ Napoleon Hill

There are times when you struggle to find content to post. We all have those days. Sometimes you just need ideas of what you can write about, so for those days here are some great resources for you:

The first resource that we use is called "Ezine Articles" - www.ezinearticles.com

This is a great place to get inspiration for posts or videos.

It is easy to add this to your Google+ posts.

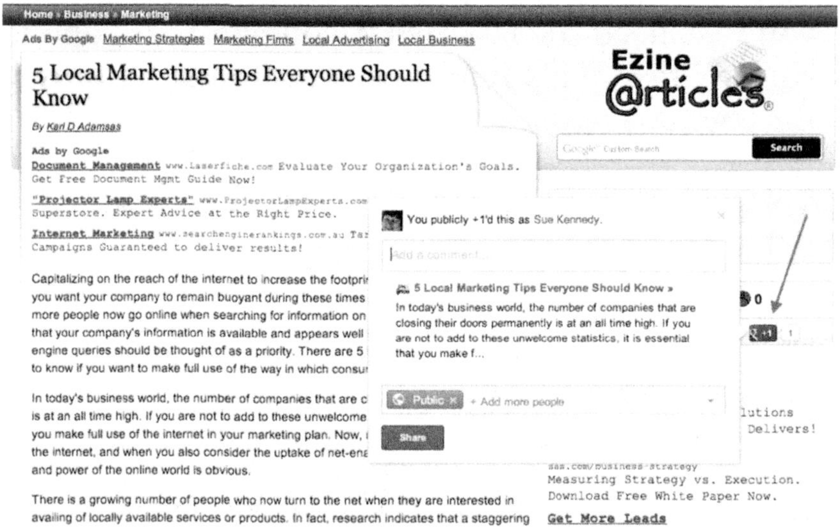

Add a comment to the article and then select which Circle you wish to post it to.

The second resource that we use is called "All-Top" - www.alltop.com

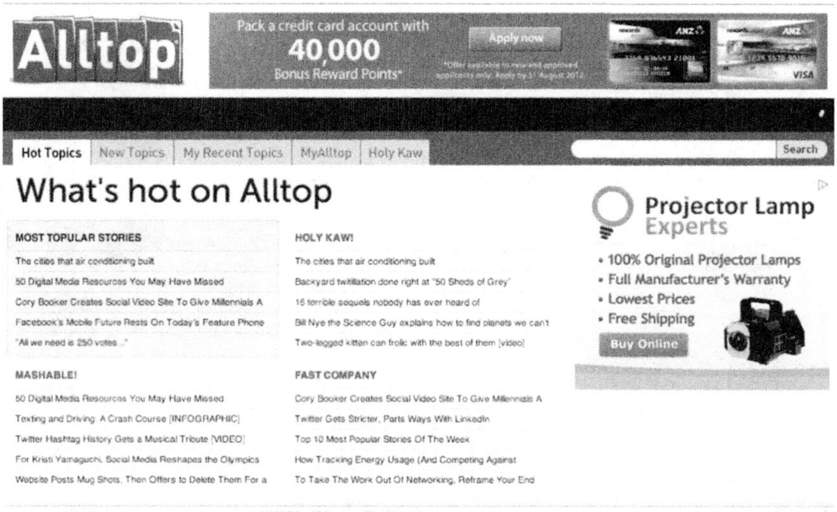

TIP: When using someone else's content in a video ALWAYS make sure you give the author credit for their work

As you can see sharing content on AllTop is also very easy.

Within Google+ is our other resource that is great.

On your home page type in your search term in the search bar.

A stream of posts will appear that other people have posted, here you can elect to share these and give credit to their work whilst building a relationship with this people.

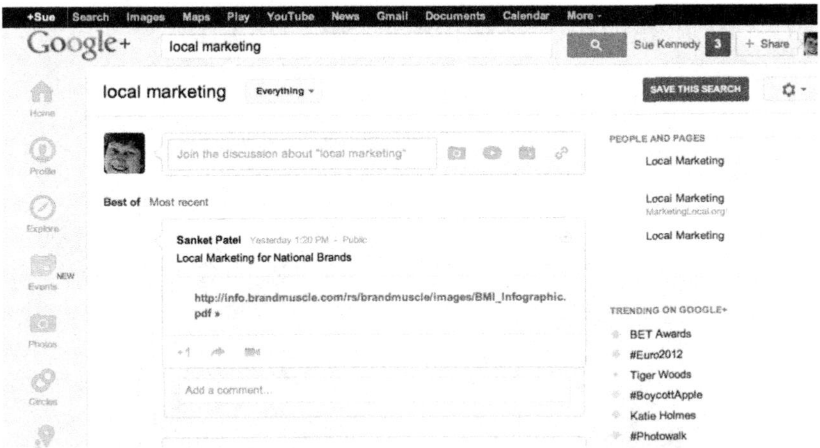

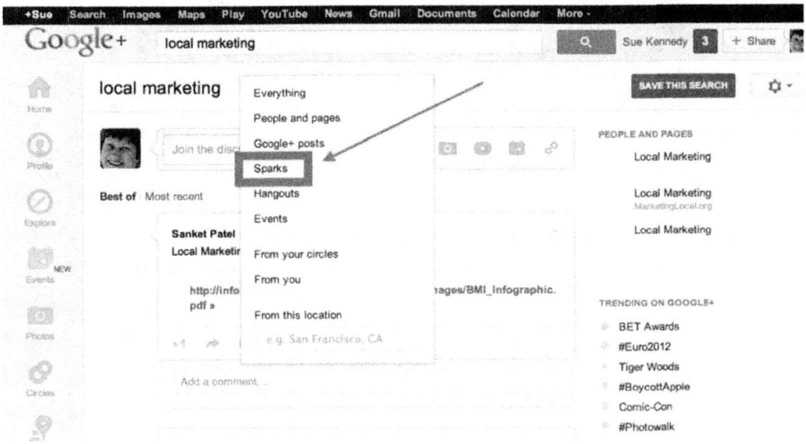

The next resource is finding content in "Sparks", this is the same as Google Alerts. This is content that Google has deemed relevant and is current.

Share these and add your commentary to the post, always select posts that have videos or photos for more effect.

Post at least once a day for best results

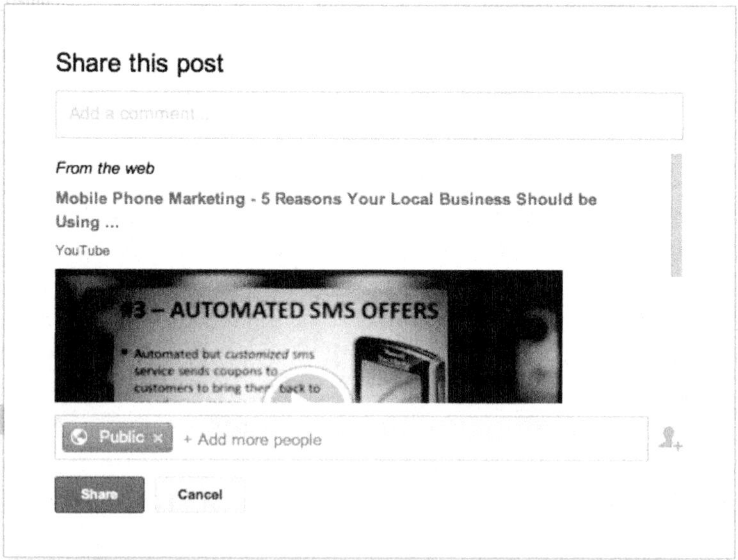

ACTION STEPS

1. Go to Ezine Articles and share a post
2. Go to AllTop and share a post
3. Go to Sparks and share a post

How to Increase your Google+ Page Value

"People are best convinced by things they themselves discover" ~ *Ben Franklin*

Following are some different ways you can increase your Google+ Page value:

- Actively use Google Hangouts (video chat drop-in)
- Maintain a daily presence via Google+
- Update and add to your Google+ Circles
- Upload YouTube videos and post the links on your page and websites
- Upload videos to Google+ and share them via your page.

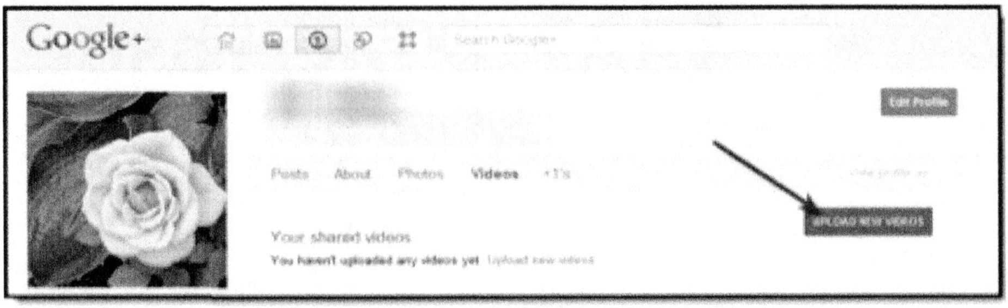

<u>Move your Google+ Page fans directly into your Circles</u>. (This seems to create automatic engagement!)

Make sure you have a Circle named "Following".

Remember: The more active you are via Google+, the higher value Google's algorithm currently seems to ascribe.

Make sure your site contains the "+1" button, as well as your badge or icon. (This will require a separate snippet of code to that of badges/icons.)

Publicise your page. Share it with your Circles and Hangouts. Share it on social networks and in your blog posts and forum posts. Include it as part of your contact information.

Upload photos, as well as videos.

ACTION STEPS

1. Try out some of the suggestions in this chapter to increase your page value

How to use Google+ for Business

"I had to make my own living and my own opportunity! But I made it! Don't sit down and wait for the opportunities to come. Get up and make them! " ~ C.J. Walker

Following are step-by-step instructions for how to set up and optimise your Google+ business page as well as the best practices to use in order to generate more buzz around your company.

TIP: Remember that it is important to set up your profile effectively BEFORE adding any business pages. The reason is that pages have LESS capabilities at this stage than your profile

10 Quick Facts About Google+

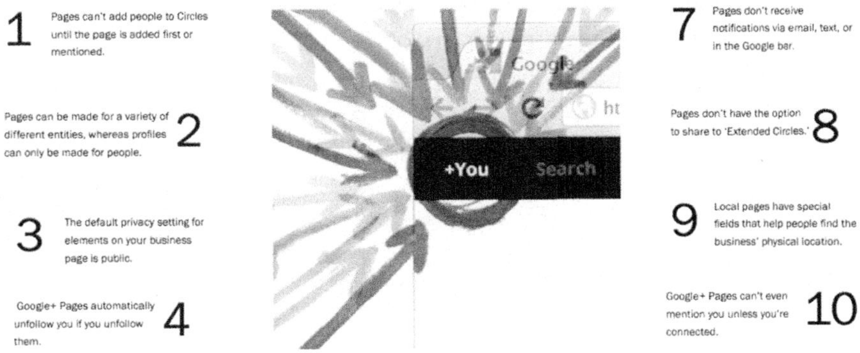

Step by Step Guide

Step 1. Choose an Accessible Gmail Account

Avoid creating your business page through just any old account, such as a personal gmail account. Instead, choose a gmail account that is accessible to multiple members of your marketing team (e.g. companymarketingteam@ gmail.com), and use that account to create your page.

Step 2. Create a page with the desired Account

Visit https://plus.google.com/pages/create and if you see the option to create a Google+ page, get started! Follow the wizard (it's much like facebook's page creation wizard), and choose the most appropriate option to classify your business as shown in the next image.

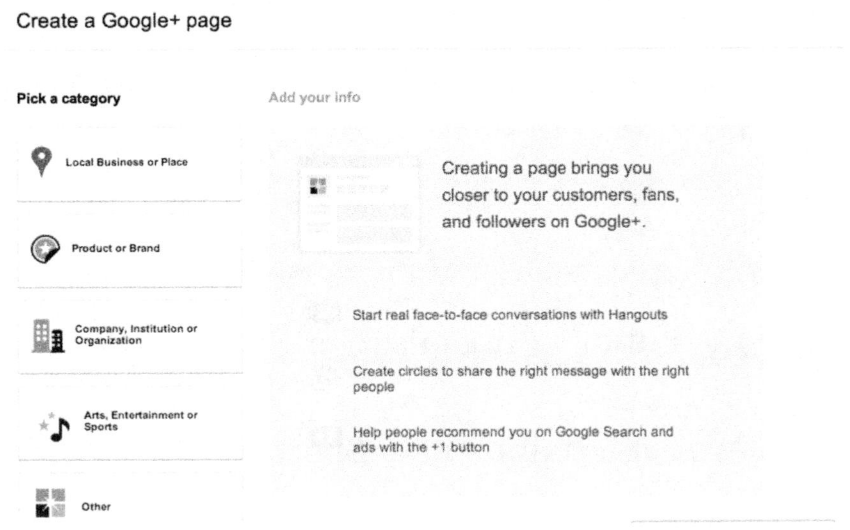

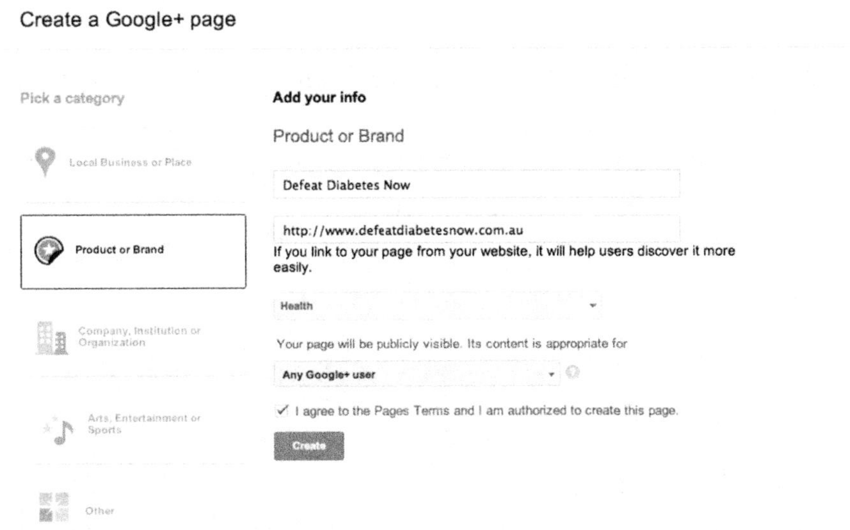

You'll be able to select from the following options:

- local Business or place
- product or Brand
- company
- Institution or organisation
- Arts, entertainment or Sports
- Other

After selecting your classification, fill in your basic information, including your page name (i.e. your company name), your business' website Url, your category (i.e. your industry), and the classification of your page's content (i.e. any Google+ user, 18 years of age or older, etc.).

Step 3. Customise Your Public Profile

The third step involves customising your public profile. The profile basics include your tagline (think of it as your business' elevator pitch) and an image (your company logo is a great option). Keep it concise, yet descriptive.

Step 4. Promote your page

At this point, you've created the skeleton of your page, and Google+ will now prompt you to promote your page. Our recommendation is to customise your page even further and start sharing a few updates before you begin telling the world about it.

Promoting a blank page isn't a great way to convince people that your page is valuable enough to add to their circles. So invest some time into optimising your page and sharing a few links of valuable content before you start promoting it to the masses.

Step 5. Optimise further

At the most basic level, this is really all you need to do to get your page launched. But as any smart marketer knows, the 'basics' aren't usually enough. Intelligent marketers understand the importance of optimising their page to make it not only more engaging, but also more valuable and effective for lead generation.

Make sure you optimise your page with keywords!

Regularly share fresh content, react and respond to your fans, be engaging, and optimise for lead generation. Then measure, adapt your strategy, and optimise your presence based on your own individual results and goals.

You need to leverage your personal brand first BEFORE your business page.

ACTION STEPS

1. Create a gmail if you don't already have one
2. Create a Google+ page with this email
3. Customise your public profile
4. List 10 ways you can use Google+ for your business

5 Handy Tips for Managing Your Google+ Business Page

"If you are not willing to risk the unusual, you will have to settle for the ordinary"
~ Jim Rohn

Even at the most basic level, the previous 5 steps will help you build your page and get it launched, but like any good business owner would know, that the basics are never enough.

It is therefore important that you further optimise your page so that it will be more engaging, valuable and effective for your followers and customers.

Here are 5 handy tips that will help you manage your Google+ business page:

Preview your page as your customers would

To see how your Google+ Page appears to the

public, toggle your view using the "View profile as" feature in the top navigation of your page. You can also type in a specific user's name to see how your page appears for that user.

Manage your page by inviting others to help

Invite team members to help manage your Google+ Page. Anyone who can help answer questions, share content, or monitor should be asked to help.

Share your content directly to communities

Google Communities are an active and engaging place for sharing content. They work just like LinkedIn Groups. You can share content into these communities right from your Google+ Page by adding them via the plus (+) feature in a status update.

While communities are an important and engaging place to share content, remember not to use this feature to spam these communities. Only share what is truly relevant and beneficial to these communities. A great idea would be to start a conversation and get a relationship forming.

Include hashtags to allow your posts to be found easily

Google+ automatically adds hashtags to posts based on the content of the update. You can also include your own hashtags (or choose to remove those added for you) this helps store your content into conversations happening in the Google+ space around that same topic.

Add visuals in your content sharing

Google+ is a highly visual network. Aside from the colossal cover image on your business page, it allows you to share images of varying formats, sizes, and styles. The Google+ algorithm then goes to work to present content in a multi-column design that adapts visual presentation based on screen size and orientation. It is well worth investing the time to use visuals when you are sharing content.

ACTION STEPS

1. Do each of the five handy tips mentioned in this chapter

How to Optimise your Business Presence on Google+

"The longer you're not taking action the more money you're losing"~ Carrie Wilkerson

Following are the 6 best Practices for marketing on Google+.

Google+ is similar to other social networks when it comes to marketing, but it does have its own strengths and weaknesses. To get the most from your Google+ Business Page in terms of traffic and leads for your business, follow these best practices:

Step One – Share lots of photos

Step Two – Add recommended links

Step Three – Promote your Google+ page on your Blog and website

Step Four – Encourage people to Share your posts

Step Five – Analyse Traffic and Leads from Google

Step Six – Use Circles to Segment Your Messages

ACTION STEPS

1. Go through each of the six steps mentioned in this chapter

Proposed uses of Google+ for Business

"The first rule of any technology used in a business is that automation applied to an efficient operation will magnify the efficiency. The second is that automation applied to an inefficient operation will magnify the inefficiency" ~ Bill Gates

Google is definitely out to create a great business page for its users.

Some of the features could include features such as a whiteboard application along with screencast abilities. There could also be a Google Meetings area as well.

Google has already made it clear that personal interaction is key. So just how will a business achieve this?

Businesses are going to need to look at Google+ as their store front.

They can create Circles such as Customers, Employees, Products, Customer Service and

Suppliers. This gives them the ability to share relevant information with each circle.

For instance you could notify your customers of special offers, deals and freebies.

You can send your employees information about vacations and human resource issues.

No one is going to feel bombarded with information overload or receiving too many marketing messages.

Google already has in place many Google applications which millions of people use. Their aim is to get businesses to use them too.

This includes having people create Gmail accounts, using Google Docs, Google Checkout, Google Adwords and Google Maps and Places.

The possibility of directly integrating these apps into Google+ is there. We will have to wait and see exactly what Google chooses to do.

One key point to consider is that Google has built its reputation on helping users find what they need. While Facebook focuses on connecting you with your friends.

So if Google does decide to integrate your business into their tools Facebook had better watch out!

A business could use Google Sparks to pull in interesting information surrounding their business and make it available to their Circles.

Hangouts, this will be a huge business potential. Already companies such as Dell want to use Hangouts as a Customer Service method.

They can enable video chat and deal with customer issues face to face. Hangouts could also be used as an instructional method.

Inviting customers to come and learn the features of certain products or items.

Some journalists are using Google+ as a way to showcase their daily jobs and gives viewers a glimpse inside the newsroom via a Hangout.

Other people are hosting daily caption competitions and posting questions on certain topics to get feedback.

Holding group discussions in your circles is another way to discover what people are looking for in different ways. You can find out their interests, what they have on their wish list and more.

ACTION STEPS

1. Make a list of different ways your business could utilise these proposed changes, for example, setting up a Hangout where you can assist your customers/clients with any problems they may have

8 SIMPLE STEPS TO MAXIMISE SEO ON GOOGLE+

"Whatever the mind of man can conceive and believe, it can achieve. Thoughts are things! And powerful things at that, when mixed with definiteness of purpose, and burning desire, can be translated into riches" ~ Napoleon Hill

Because Google+ is only in it's infancy, you need to keep in mind that you need to implement a unique marketing strategy so that you can benefit as much as possible.

Please find below 8 steps that will help you get your content the best advantage when it comes to SEO. This will help you increase your visibility of your posts and gives your social media marketing strategy a boost that will only benefit you in the long run.

1. Set all your posts to "Public".

Having more circles can create a broader interest for your friends, but by telling Google that all of your posts can be shared publicly will allow them to be indexed in the public search engine. Every time you post, select the Public option.

2. Use a source link when adding your content to Google+.

Google+ has not been playing well with URL shorteners, so when possible use a link directly from the source. This helps Google more efficiently populate your content, including the name of your blog, post title, description and image. The content will also be cross-referenced with any +1 "likes" from other Google+ users. Much like sharing URLs through other social media sites, you just copy and paste the original link to the "Share what's new" box on your homepage.

3. Add a "+" before a person's name in order to link to their profile in a post.

Anyone that you are connected to on Google+ can be linked in the same way as on your Facebook network. A feature that some users are unaware of; this lets you do this by simply prefixing the name with a "+" as you write your post. This will highlight the name, letting readers view the individual's profile, that is, if privacy settings allow it. Being able to link with others helps open conversations and engages users.

4. Be sure to broaden your circles, add friends, engage and share.

Like Facebook, the more you engage others, the longer your posts will remain visible to other users. Increasing the number of people in your circles to share with will give your content more reach.

5. Spread the +1 button around all of your sites.

The small piece of code is easy to embed on all of your web pages, blogs, e-commerce sites, etc. The easier it is for readers to click on your share buttons, the more likely it is that they will do so. Easy sharing helps extend the reach of your content through social media.

6. Fill out your profile as completely as you feel comfortable.

Over time, your Google profile will create itself depending on choices that you make. By adding other touches to it, you will grow your profile and curate it so that it fits you perfectly. Take a look at your social media profile and decide what areas you feel need more information added. The more open you are on your public profiles, the better.

7. Consider clicking the "Email people not using Google+" for some of your best posts.

If you are connected with people who are not on Google+ yet, you can still share your content with them by having an email sent directly to them. This is not an option you should choose for everything, as this can cause you to become an annoyance. Instead, only choose to do this when you have written a great piece of content that you want to send out there.

8. Take part in the Google+ community.

How much you actively participate on Google+ can affect your relevance on this social media site. How many people you reach can help you become ranked higher.

Making the most of Google+ takes patience and commitment. When you do it right, the rewards you reap will be worth the effort you make.

ACTION STEPS

1. Make sure you do each of the eight steps mentioned in this chapter to achieve maximum SEO benefits

Understanding Google+ Local scores

"I wasn't satified just to earn a good living. I was looking to make a statement" ~ Donald Trump

All scores in Google+ Local are determined by user reviews.

Individual user ratings are based on a 0 to 3 point scale as shown here:

3 Excellent
2 Very Good
1 Good
0 Poor to Fair

Google takes the ratings, averages them, and then multiplies by ten to arrive at an **average score**.

•What do the Scores Mean?

26-30 Extraordinary to perfection
21-25 Very good to excellent
16-20 Good to very good

10-15 Fair to good
0-9 Poor to fair

Google+ Vocabulary: A Quick Reference Glossary

"Don't think of Google+ as yet another social site to deal with. Think of it as the only social site you hav e to deal with."
~ Mike Elgan, Founder, Writer, Columnist, and Blogger at Elgan Media

Google+ Glossary

Mike Elgan, a writer, columnist, and blogger has over two million followers on Google+, he explains how this social network works as follows:

"Instead of saying, "I'm going to write a blog post now," or "I'm going to send an email" or "I think I'll tweet something" you simply say what you have to say, then decide who you're going to say it to.

- If you address it to 'Public,' it's a blog post.
- If you address it to 'Your Circles,' it's a tweet.

- If you address it to your 'My Customers' Circle, it's a business newsletter.
- If you address it to a single person, it can be a letter to your mother.

"I'd say this is pretty revolutionary."

With that in mind, let's take a look at some of the terms he references, as well as others, to help you understand the various features available on Google+

GOOGLE+ KEY TERMS AND FEATURES

+1 Button: The equivalent of the Facebook Like button for Google+ and Google Search. A user can +1 an item shared on Google+ as well as a search engine result link returned by a Google search.

Chat: A method for sending short messages to other Google+ members who are also signed in to Google+.

Circle: The method of organising connections into groups for more targeted sharing and better privacy.

Comment: A response to a user's Google+ post.

Community: Environments on Google+ where users can gather and discuss shared interests (similar to LinkedIn Groups).

Event: Fully customisable Google+ pages for inviting Google+ users and community members to a particular event. Google+ automatically adds these events to attendee Google Calendars.

Google+ Page: A digital platform for a business or organisation to share content related to their brand.

Google Profile: Your personal home on Google+, which allows you to share interesting work experiences, personal information, and much more.

Hangout: A platform for group video chatting and collaboration that is used by Google+ members, with a maximum participation allowance of 10 users. Hangouts can also be broadcasted live to a public audience and automatically recorded to YouTube.

Share: Allows you to share a message that someone else created with your followers (similar to a retweet on Twitter).

Stream: The list of real-time messages that are displayed on the Google+ home screen and for each Circle of contacts. Google+ streams are responsive, adapting to the screen size and orientation of browsers.

Conclusion

*"Good business leaders create a vision,
articulate the vision,
passionately own the vision,
and relentlessly drive it to completion"
~ Jack Welch*

In this book we have discussed the basics. Ultimately, any social media marketing involves staying up-to-date with the various features that get released, and it all comes back to building real relationships with real people.

Google+ offers another platform to share relevant content and conversation. Google's version of a social network lets you tap into a community-based site like LinkedIn with a visual, share-happy angle like Facebook.

There's just no time for a business owner marketing their products and/or services to be lazy and stand on a soapbox in the corner shouting about his or her business. You can't simply push content or push agendas into a place like Google+ and expect any success at all. However, you can if you do it right.

If you know how to work a room then you will understand the need to add value by sharing helpful content, by asking questions and responding to them, and by generally being a good person to others you encounter on any of your social networks.

As for Google+ specifically, between a growing community of potential visitors to your site, a strong tie to SEO on Google.com, and a platform where you can publish, share, and interact based on shared interests, it's easy to see more and more how your business can benefit from the development of strategies around this network.

Your success will come not because of the simple presence of your page, but because you will know that practicing the strategies you learnt in this book means you are adding value and helping customers find what they're truly seeking when they are looking to buy:

A business – YOUR business – which helps and makes their lives better can only mean success!

That really does deserve a great BIG +1...

Questions you really need to ask yourself and Actions you need to take:

- **Do you realise the magnitude of Google+ for your business?**
- **Are you serious about your business?**
- **Is your Website & Social Media Profiles optimised properly?**
- **Do you want the ability of staying in front of your competitors at all times?**

ABOUT THE AUTHOR

Sue Kennedy is an author and consultant.

Sydney Web Consultants is all about helping businesses utilise the internet with effective online marketing strategies that will allow you to create a web presence so your business can grow and prosper. All facets of Online Marketing strategies are a vital tool for your business if you want to succeed. The future lies with the internet, so being able to market your business effectively with online marketing strategies is an essential tool for your business. We have various services available to suit your individual requirements.

It is important to remember that online advertising is what works today and will continue to grow in the future. Do you want your business to get left behind or will you take the essential step and move forward with today's technology? A smart business decision is to invest in a strategic online marketing consultant to take care of all your online needs, and this is where Sydney Web Consultants can help you and your business.

<u>Our Expertise</u>

- Complete Market & Website Analysis - holistic & comprehensive
- Expertise – developed over 700 websites in every niche
- 20+ years combined "real world" business experience

<u>Our Approach</u>

- We help business owners gain more customers and sales. Plain and simple.
- The ways we do that are unique to each client. Even two clients in the same industry but different markets will be handled differently.
- Competitive analysis, market analysis, niche analysis, and analysis of each client's assets and collaterals
- We specialise in Search Engine Optimisation and Web Marketing (Video, Articles, Press Releases, etc.)
- We offer clear benefits for your bottom line

- We can make your site Search Engine Friendly, Mobile Ready and Super-Easy to Update
- We Offer no hard pitches, hype nor tricks... Just Two Questions:

1. ***What do you want your online business to accomplish?***
2. ***In your market, what's the best way to achieve that?***

<u>Only 2% of Your Market May Know Who You Are</u>

Imagine Your Profits After the 98% Catches On!

<u>Services Provided:</u>

- Web Design and Development
- Custom Facebook Fan Pages
- Facebook Applications
- Copywriting & Sales Pages, Squeeze (Landing) Pages
- Mobile Marketing
- On-Page SEO
- Off-Page SEO
- Mobile Websites
- Mobile Applications
- Article Writing for your website or blog
- Press Releases
- Keyword Research Reports

- Video Creation and Marketing
- Google Places Local Listings
- Social Media Management
- Content Creation
- If the service you are after is not listed above, please do not hesitate to contact us and ask – it is more likely than not that we can help

Offices in Sydney, Australia and Los Angeles, U.S.

Online Success in Business is Connecting Your Market to Your Website

How Can We Help You?

Sue@SydneyWebConsultants.com.au

1300 36 77 27

Printed in Dunstable, United Kingdom

91219600R00070